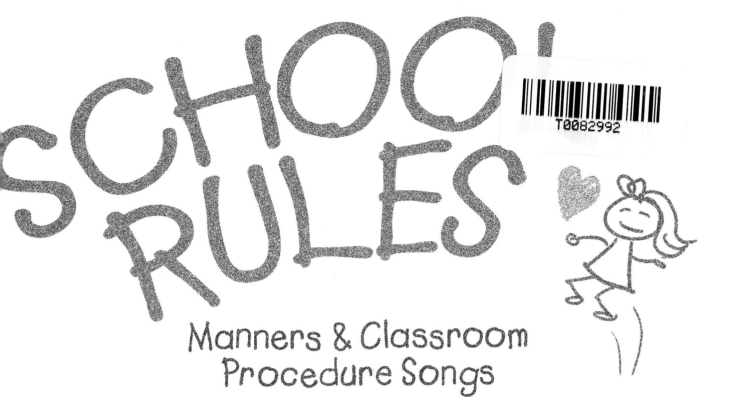

SCHOOL RULES

Manners & Classroom Procedure Songs

By Brad Green

HAL•LEONARD® CORPORATION

7777 W. BLUEMOUND RD. P.O. BOX 13819 MILWAUKEE, WI 53213

Visit Hal Leonard Online at
www.halleonard.com

TABLE OF CONTENTS

Title   Page

INTRODUCTION

School Rules — Manners and Classroom Procedure Songs is a collection of songs about rules, manners, and classroom procedures. It provides an exciting way for students to quickly learn and remember common rules. Research indicates that "music is a powerful carrier of signals that activate emotion and long-term memory." (Webb & Webb, 1990) When instructions are sung, children remember them better! Students may quickly "tune out" a spoken voice, but a song or rhyme has intrinsic appeal.

There are many options for using these songs. The teacher can use them 1) for lesson transitions to move seamlessly from one event to the next, 2) to begin and end each day or lesson, or 3) to help remind students of a certain behavior or procedure.

The music specialist can use the Musical Activities section to teach music skills and concepts, planning the songs and activities as a single activity or expanded into an entire lesson. The classroom teacher can correlate the songs to other subjects by using the Cross-Curricular Activities section. It is best if the two teachers work in tandem and reinforce the learning of the songs in both settings.

Make the songs in *School Rules* your own! Sing as much or as little of the song as you wish. For example, if students have formed a circle before you finish "Make A Circle," it is not necessary to finish. If the students have not finished making a circle by the end of the song, sing it again. Change the words to fit the current situation.

I want to thank Dr. Susan Brumfield, the great people at Hal Leonard, and my wife and daughter. I gratefully dedicate this book to the teachers who use ideas like these in their classrooms. Effective classrooms happen because of gifted and experienced teachers. I am indebted to the teachers who have shared their "tricks of the trade" with me.

ABOUT THE WRITER

BRAD GREEN is a composer, arranger and teacher. He received a B. M. in Theory and Composition from Ouachita Baptist University, an M. M. in Composition from Southwestern Baptist Theological Seminary, and is currently pursuing a Ph. D. in Music Education at Texas Tech University.

Before beginning doctoral studies, Brad was an elementary and middle school music teacher in the Fort Worth ISD and director of children's choirs in several Texas churches.

Brad Green has become known for his exciting folksong arrangements, and original works. He is an experienced Kodaly educator and is a member of the Music Educators National Conference, the Organization of American Kodály Educators, and the Texas Music Educators Association. He enjoys co-writing music with his wife Lucy and teaching his daughter, Maggie, new songs.

Webb, D., & Webb, T. (1990) *Accelerated Learning with Music.* Norcross, GA: Accelerated Learning Systems.

1. ALWAYS SHARE

(2-measure introduction on recording)

Words and Music by BRAD GREEN

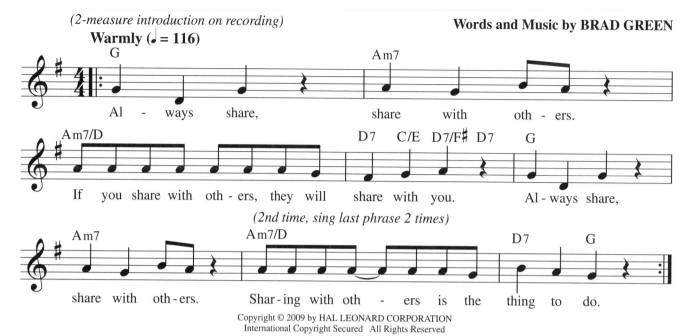

Warmly (♩ = 116)

Al - ways share, share with oth - ers.

If you share with oth - ers, they will share with you. Al - ways share,

(2nd time, sing last phrase 2 times)

share with oth - ers. Shar - ing with oth - ers is the thing to do.

Teacher Tips

When to Use the Song
- To teach the concept of sharing
- When students need to be encouraged or reminded to share

Rule/Procedure
Sharing, manners

Brief Version
Sing the words of the first four or the last four measures, using the melody of the last four measures.

Similar Songs
#18   The Golden Rule
#34   Show Respect
#45   When You Use Good Manners

Musical Activities
- Identify the phrases that are the same.
- Pat the steady beat while singing the song.
- Students create motions that represent sharing.
- Perform these motions to the beat of the song.
- Substitute the word "share" with another behavior while singing the song.

Cross-Curricular Activities

Reading
- Lead students to find the rhyming words. *(you, to, do)*
- Place several words from the song on board/overhead or speak them aloud. Have students determine if the words presented have one or two syllables.

Writing
- Have students write a paragraph about why sharing is a good behavior.
- Have students write a story about themselves in a situation when sharing was (is) difficult.

Math
Teach division (and sharing) by splitting an apple (or other objects) into parts.

Social Studies
Guide students in a discussion of what things are commonly shared. What things are shared in the classroom or in the home?

2. BE CAREFUL

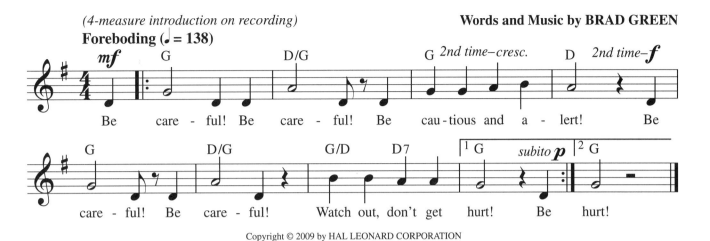

(4-measure introduction on recording)

Words and Music by BRAD GREEN

Foreboding (♩ = 138)

Be care - ful! Be care - ful! Be cau - tious and a - lert! Be care - ful! Be care - ful! Watch out, don't get hurt! Be hurt!

 Teacher Tips

When to Use the Song

- When moving to or from recess, the cafeteria, or another class
- When going on a field trip
- When playing a game
- Any activity where children need to be careful

Rule/Procedure

Being careful, being cautious

Brief Version

Sing the last four measures with the pick-up note.

Similar Songs

#41   Walk, Don't Run!

Musical Activities

- Lead the students in a conducting activity: Conduct this song and discover where the strong beats fall. Does the word "care" fall on a strong beat? *(yes)* Does the word "be" fall on a strong beat? *(no)*

- The word "be" falls on the weak beat, and is called an *anacrusis* (or pick-up). It usually appears on the weak beat directly before the strong beat. Sing the song again, and direct students to snap for the weak beat on the word "be" and clap for the strong beat on the word "care."

Cross-Curricular Activities

Reading
Have students learn to read and spell the words "careful," "cautious" and "alert."

Language Arts
Define *synonym*. Have students find at least two synonyms in this song. *(careful, cautious, alert)*

Writing
- Have students find other synonyms for the word "careful."

- Have students write a story about a time when they were not careful, and what happened to them as a result.

Social Studies
- This song is about being cautious and alert. Discuss ways that one can be cautious in class, in the hall, or on the playground.

- As a class, compile a list of ways that students can be more cautious and alert.

3. BE STILL

Words and Music by BRAD GREEN

(2-measure introduction on recording)

Quietly! (♩ = 144)

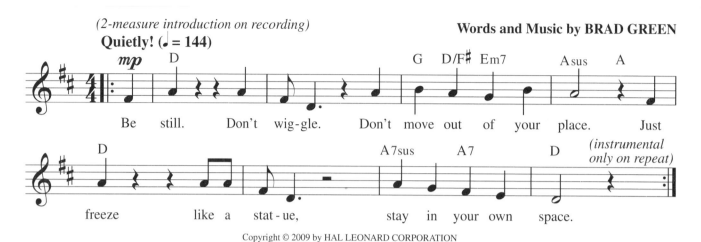

Be still. Don't wig-gle. Don't move out of your place. Just

freeze like a stat-ue, stay in your own space.

The original purchaser of this book has permission to reproduce this song for educational use in one school only. Any other use is strictly prohibited.

 Teacher Tips

When to Use the Song
To teach students the "freeze" position

Rule/Procedure
Being still

Brief Version
Sing the first two motives only:
"Be still, don't wiggle."

Similar Songs
8   Come to Attention

#12   Everybody Listen

#16   Give Me the Magic Five!

#20   Hocus Pocus, Everybody Focus

#32   Rules Song

Musical Activities
• Have students show the downward motion in the last phrase with their hands. Discuss how the melody moves to its "home tone." This final note is called *do*.

• Have students practice freezing like a statue during the singing of the song.

Cross-Curricular Activities

Reading/Language Arts
• Find the rhyming words. *(place, space)*

• Read the story *The Statue of Liberty* by Betsy Maestro and Giulio Maestro.

Writing
Look at a statue or a picture of a statue. Write a description of the statue. Where did it come from? Why does it look the way it does? What is it made of? Who made it? When was it made? Do you like it, or not? Why?

Math
Have students measure one's shadow at different times of the day (8 AM, 10 AM and 12 noon, for example). Discover that if one stands still like a statue that the movement of the sun will cause the length of the shadow to change. Measure that difference.

Social Studies
• Help students search the Internet for facts about the Statue of Liberty and other American landmarks.

• Find pictures of other famous statues.

Science
Display pictures of statues made from a variety of materials (stone, metal, marble, for example). Have students share their observations.

Art
Have students create a statue from modeling clay. Allow the clay to harden before moving or displaying the statues.

4. BEFORE YOU SPEAK, RAISE YOUR HAND

(4-measure introduction on recording)   **Words and Music by BRAD GREEN**

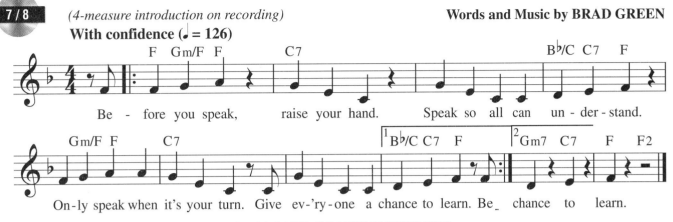

Be - fore you speak, raise your hand. Speak so all can un - der - stand.

On-ly speak when it's your turn. Give ev-'ry-one a chance to learn. Be_ chance to learn.

Teacher Tips

When to Use the Song
- To teach students to speak only during their turn, when their hand is raised
- Use this gentle reminder when students speak out of turn. Acknowledging students who speak out of turn before students who have their hand raised reinforces the idea that students *do not* have to raise their hand before they speak.

Rule/Procedure
Speaking when called on; waiting for your turn

Brief Version
Sing the first two measures only.

Similar Songs
#12 Everybody Listen

#16 Give Me the Magic Five!

#32 Rules Song

#34 Show Respect

#38 Take Turns

#45 When You Use Good Manners

Musical Activities
- Discover the melodic contour (moving up or down or staying the same) in each two-measure phrase by having students show the movement with their hands.

- Guide students to discover that the melody during "before you speak" moves in steps, and the melody for "raise your hand" moves in skips.

Cross-Curricular Activities

Reading/Language Arts
- Write the sentence "Before you speak, raise your hand." on the board. Ask students: Where is there a pause in this sentence? *(after the comma)* What punctuation is used at the end of the sentence? *(a period)*

- Introduce opposites. Discuss what is the opposite of "before." Have students create a list of opposites such as above/below, in/out, front/back, up/down.

Writing
Have students write two sentences that use opposite words. (Example: I went to the board before recess./I went to the board after recess.)

Math
With a partner, have students measure how much taller they are when their hands are raised.

Social Studies
Have students make a list of places or situations where people take turns.

Art
Apply the task of taking turns by painting a class mural. Have students take turns painting for a specified amount of time.

5. BUENOS DIAS

(4-measure introduction on recording)

Words and Music by BRAD GREEN

Teacher Tips

When to Use the Song
- For use in a Spanish or multicultural lesson
- When learning common phrases in other languages
- During a social studies or geography lesson

Rule/Procedure
Learning common Spanish greetings and their English translation

Brief Version
Sing the first eight measures only.

Similar Songs
#19 Hello
#22 It's Time to Say Goodbye
#24 Life Is Better With a Friend
#30 Please and Thank You
#44 When You Say "Hello"
#45 When You Use Good Manners

Musical Activities
- Have students create a repeating rhythmic pattern. Clap this pattern during the song.
- Play selected words with rhythm instruments. Vary the words and instruments until students can perform the entire song on rhythm instruments only.

Movement Activities
- Have half the class clap or tap the beat while the other half claps or taps the rhythm of the words while singing the song. Reverse roles.
- Divide the class into partners. Have them improvise movements (handshake, wave, high-five) to greet one another while singing the song.
- After students are familiar with the song, teach the suggested motions.

Cross-Curricular Activities

Reading/Language Arts
- Younger students: Compare the "i" vowel sound in the Spanish word "dias" with the "i" vowel sound in English words "fine" or "nice."
- Older students: Write the words "Buenos Dias" on the board. Underline the double vowels. Compare the "ue" in "Buenos" to the "ue" in English words such as "argue," "blue," "cruel," and "duet." Compare the "ia" in "dias" to the "ia" in English such as "giant," "dial," "cafeteria," and "brilliant."

Writing
Write a dialogue using the phrases in this song.

Math
- Have the students count the number of phrases in this song that they echo sing. *(8)*
- Count the number of syllables found in the phrases "Good Morning, how are you?" and, "I'm fine, thank you." *(6, 4)*

Social Studies
Lead students to discover what countries use Spanish as the primary language. Use a world map to locate these countries.

Art
Produce samples of art from Spanish-speaking countries and/or from Spanish artists.

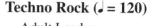

6. CLAP ONE TIME IF YOU CAN HEAR MY VOICE

(4-measure introduction on recording)

Words and Music by BRAD GREEN

Techno Rock (♩ = 120)

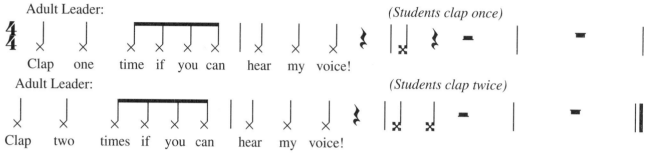

Adult Leader:

(Students clap once)

Clap one time if you can hear my voice!

Adult Leader:

(Students clap twice)

Clap two times if you can hear my voice!

Instructions: Repeat the chant as little or as often as necessary, increasing or changing the number of claps until the students reach the level of attention desired.

 Teacher Tips

When to Use the Song
When student attention is needed quickly

Rule/Procedure
Coming to attention or quieting the students quickly

Similar Songs
#8   Come to Attention

#12   Everybody Listen

#16   Give Me the Magic Five!

#20   Hocus Pocus, Everybody Focus

#32   Rules Song

#45   When You Use Good Manners

Musical Activities
• Teach different dynamic levels. Have the students sing a familiar song with different dynamic levels (loud or soft).

• Have a contest to see how quickly students can come to attention. Make it fun! Have the students talk and move around until it is time to pay attention.

• Note: Speak softly rather than loudly when you want the attention of the students.

Cross-Curricular Activities

Reading/Language Arts
• List, define, and substitute other action words for "clap" in the song.

Math
• Learn to tell time by watching the second hand. When everyone is quiet after singing this song, have class watch the clock and stay quiet for 5 seconds, then 10 seconds.

• Assign different students the task of timing how long it takes the class to complete a task (lining up to go to lunch, coming in from recess, and so forth).

Social Studies
Discuss why it is important to quickly pay attention when other people need to speak to you.

Art
Express the mood of focus, attention, solitude or quiet in a painting or drawing.

7. CLEAN UP!

(4-measure introduction on recording)

In two ($\downarrow$ = 98)

(3 times; Instrumental 3rd time)

Words and Music by BRAD GREEN

Clean up! Clean up! Stop what you're do-ing and ev-'ry-bod-y pick up, straight-en up! Let's get read-y to (*sing**). (*march*)

* Insert name of next activity.

 Teacher Tips

When to Use the Song
When cleaning up after an activity

Rule/Procedure
Cleaning up; personal responsibility

Similar Songs
#39   There Are Two Minutes Left

Musical Activities
- Insert the name of an activity at the end of the song, such as "Let's get ready to *leave*," or "Let's get ready to *read*," or "Let's get ready to *go to lunch*."
- Have students create different movements that represent "cleaning up." Perform the movement and let the other students guess what is being "cleaned up."
- Have students discover the lowest pitch in this song, the word that is sung with it, and how many times it is sung. (*C; second syllable of "everybody;" one time*)

Cross-Curricular Activities
Reading/Language Arts
Lead students to notice that the "ea" vowel sound in the words "clean" and "ready" are spelled the same, but do not sound the same. Identify other vowel combinations that are spelled the same, but do not sound the same when used in different words (for example, the "ea" in the words "peach" and "health").

Writing
This song may be used during writing class by adapting the words. Sing "Stop now. Stop now. Stop what you're doing and everybody look up. Look at me. How much did you write?"

Math
Practice counting by conducting a clean-up contest. Have students count how many items they can clean or pick up in a specified amount of time.

Social Studies
- Identify things in the school or at home that need to be cleaned and/or maintained. Who is responsible for keeping them clean or maintained? How much are we as individuals responsible to take care of public/shared things?
- Discuss personal responsibility and how important it is to clean up after ourselves at home, at school, or any place.

Science
Use this song to lead into a lesson on recycling. Recognize the students who develop the most creative recycling ideas.

8. COME TO ATTENTION

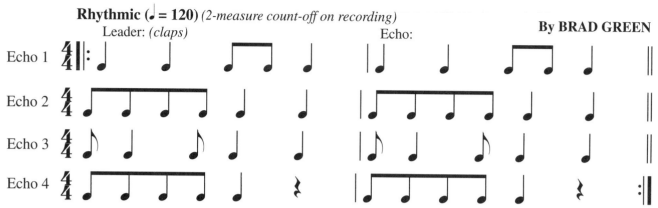

Rhythmic ($\quarternote$ = 120) *(2-measure count-off on recording)*

By BRAD GREEN

Continue using echoes until you have all the students' attention.

Teacher Tips

When to Use the Song
- When student attention is needed quickly
- To quiet students quickly

Rule/Procedure
- Coming to attention
- Practicing listening skills

Similar Songs
6   Clap Once If You Can Hear My Voice
#12   Everybody Listen
#16   Give Me the Magic Five!
#20   Hocus Pocus, Everybody Focus
#32   Rules Song

Musical Activities
- Perform the rhythmic patterns with other body percussion such as pat the knees, tap the top of head, tap the elbow, stomp a foot, snap the fingers, and so forth.
- Change and create new rhythmic patterns, and students echo.
- Play a game called "Rhythm Round." Teacher claps a 4-beat rhythmic pattern. Students echo. During the student echo, teacher presents a new pattern on a different part of the body. Teacher is always four beats ahead of students. This pattern continues with the teacher presenting a new 4-beat pattern for the students, who are imitating one pattern while watching the teacher to see the new pattern. For older students, teacher may lengthen the rhythmic pattern to eight beats.
- For more advanced students divide the students into three or more groups that imitate each other. The teacher performs a 4-beat pattern, and the first group imitates the teacher, then the second group imitates the first group when they finish, and so on.
- Have students analyze the pattern of the first echo (long, long, short-short, long), and then the others. Are any two the same? *(no)*

Cross-Curricular Activities

Math
Have students count the number of times they clap for each echo, and then add then up. Change the patterns to change the count.

Social Studies
This activity communicates a message without words. Discuss other ways that humans communicate without words.

Science
Analyze the sounds created by various body percussion movements (tap, clap, stomp). Why do they sound differently?

9. CRISS-CROSS APPLESAUCE

(thanks to Priscila Dilley for this song idea)

(4-measure introduction on recording)

Words and Music by BRAD GREEN

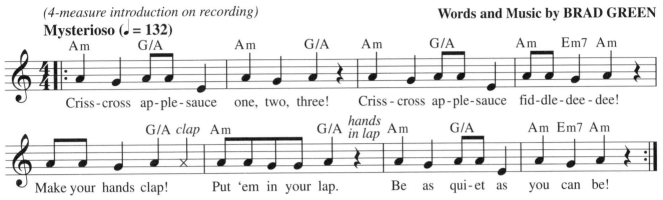

 Teacher Tips

When to Use the Song

Students, especially young children, need guidance when sitting on the floor in large groups. This song is an easy way to instruct them on how to sit neatly, and the motions of the song encourage them to be still.

Rule/Procedure

Sitting on the floor neatly with hands to yourself

Brief Version

Sing the first measure.

Similar Songs

#14   Follow the Instructions

#17   Go Back to Your Place

#23   Keep Your Hands to Yourself

#31   Polka Dot Spot

#36   Stand Up/Sit Down

#37   Stay in Your Seat

Musical Activities

- Discuss major and minor. This song is in a minor mode because it begins and ends on *la*, but can be sung in a major mode. Play "A-C-E" triad (A minor) and then "A-C-sharp-E" triad (A major) on piano, barred instruments, or Autoharp. Sing the song once playing the A minor chord and then again playing the A major chord. Compare the two.

- Have students sing other songs in this book that are in a minor mode (#33 "Say Your Name" and #11 "Don't Forget Your Homework").

- Count the phrases in this song. *(measures 1-2, 3-4, 5-6, 7-8 or 4 total)* Which phrase has motions? *(phrase 3 or measures 5 & 6)*

Cross-Curricular Activities

Reading/Language Arts

Ask students what the words "applesauce" or "fiddle-dee-dee" mean in this song. *(nothing)* Use the opportunity to discuss nonsense words. Make a list words we use everyday that are nonsense words.

Math

Word problem. "If it takes two legs for one person to sit criss-cross, how many legs would take for 10 people to sit criss-cross? 20 people? 30 people?"

Social Studies

Why is it important to stay in one's own place? Where are some places where people have to sit in an assigned space? *(in desks, airplane, sporting events)*

Science

Investigate and discover how apples become applesauce.

Art

Create a picture using only the letter "x" (a tiny criss-cross). Similar to pointillism, only use the letter "x" instead of dots.

10. DO YOU HAVE WHAT YOU NEED?

(2-measure introduction on recording)

Words and Music by BRAD GREEN

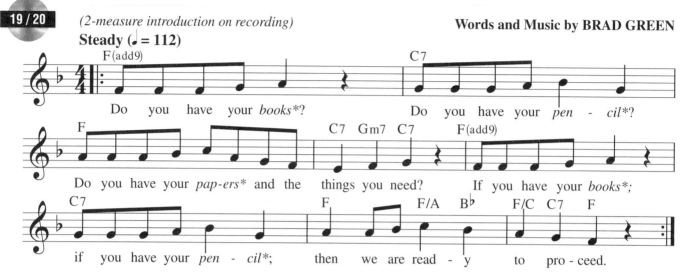

Do you have your *books**? Do you have your *pen - cil**?

Do you have your *pap-ers** and the things you need? If you have your *books**;

if you have your *pen - cil**; then we are read - y to pro - ceed.

* Substitute "books" and "pencil" for any supplies or materials needed for the activity.

Teacher Tips

When to Use the Song
When starting a new activity

Rule/Procedure
Being prepared

Brief Version
Sing the first two measures.

Similar Songs
#11   Don't Forget Your Homework

#15   Get Ready to Start the Day

#46   You'll Need Your (Book) for This Activity

Musical Activities
Determine the form. Teacher sings each two-measure phrase and students echo. Then, lead students to determine which phrases are the same and which ones are different. Label the first phrase "a." Sing the second phrase (children echo). The same or different? *(different)*. Label this phrase "b." Sing third phrase. Same or different? *(same as first phrase)*. Label third phrase "a." Sing final phrase. *(different from the others)*. Label the last phrase "c." Form of the song is abac.

Cross-Curricular Activities:

Reading/Language Arts
Write the question "Do you have your books?" on the board. Teach the use of the question mark. Learn more about punctuation by having students read *Punctuation Takes a Vacation* by Robin Pulver and Lynn Rowe Reed.

Writing
Write an account of a time when you were unprepared because you did not have what you needed. Share how that made you feel.

Math
Determine the number of sheets of paper needed for "x" number of activities per day. From that, calculate how many sheets needed for 5 days, 20 days, and 180 days.

Social Studies
Discuss careers. Determine what materials are needed for a specific career.

Science
Make a list of materials needed before one can proceed to do today's science activity.

Art
Construct a container to hold "the things you need" for an activity, such as a collage pencil box.

11. DON'T FORGET YOUR HOMEWORK

(4-measure introduction on recording)

Words and Music by BRAD GREEN

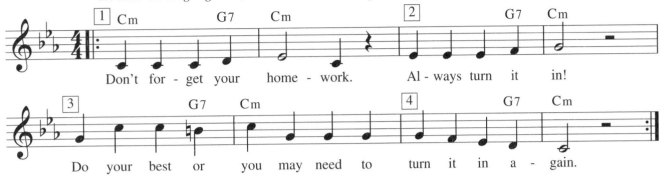

With angst (♩ = 126)

1st time–all sing together; 2nd & 3rd times–sing as a 4-part round

Don't for - get your home - work. Al - ways turn it in!

Do your best or you may need to turn it in a - gain.

Teacher Tips

When to Use the Song

- To remind students, especially at the end of the day, to complete their homework.

- When reminding students of a test, supplies, or forms that are due. Change the words to fit a particular situation. Example: "Don't forget your picture money. It's time to turn it in."

Rule/Procedure

Remembering assignments

Similar Songs

#10   Do You Have What You Need?

#22   It's Time to Say Goodbye

#40   Toodle-Oodle-Oo

#46   You'll Need Your *(Book)* for This Activity

Musical Activities

- Sing this song in a 2-, 3-, or 4-part canon.

- Add an instrumental accompaniment by composing a four-beat pattern on the notes C and G.

- This song is in a minor mode because it begins and ends on *la*. Have students sing other songs in this book that are in a minor mode such as #33 - "Say Your Name."

Movement Activities

Have students create movements for each phrase and perform the movements in canon.

Cross-Curricular Activities

Reading/Language Arts

This song tells students to "do your best or you may need to turn it in again." Lead students in a discussion about proofreading. The first draft may not be the best. Share proofreading tips such as reading the words aloud or letting someone else read the words to check for mistakes.

Writing

Help students write a first draft and revise their work. Lead a discussion on why revision is important.

Math

Instruct student to practice checking their math homework alone or with a partner before turning it in.

Social Studies

Lead students in a discussion about doing their best. Homework is where we can practice doing our best while working by ourselves. What are some other skills that we must practice several times before we can do our best? *(sports, hobbies, writing, foreign languages, musical instruments, and so forth)*

12. EVERYBODY LISTEN

(4-measure introduction on recording)

Words and Music by BRAD GREEN

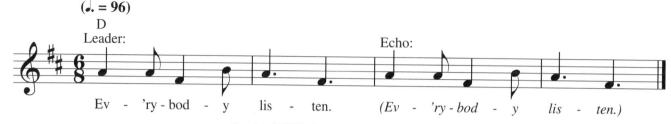

Ev - 'ry - bod - y lis - ten. *(Ev - 'ry - bod - y lis - ten.)*

Copyright © 2009 by HAL LEONARD CORPORATION
International Copyright Secured   All Rights Reserved

 **Teacher Tips**

When to Use the Song
To quickly get student attention

Rule/Procedure
- Coming to attention or quieting the students quickly
- Practicing listening skills

Similar Songs
#8   Come to Attention
#16   Give Me the Magic Five!
#20   Hocus Pocus, Everybody Focus
#32   Rules Song

Musical Activities
Sing this song at different dynamic levels, and present the corresponding musical symbols:

ff – *fortissimo* – very loud

f – *forte* – loud

mf – *mezzo forte* – moderately loud

mp – *mezzo piano* – moderately soft

p – *piano* – soft

pp – *pianissimo* – very soft

Cross-Curricular Activities

Reading/Language Arts
"Listen" is an action verb. Make a list of other action verbs. When appropriate, substitute these new verbs for "listen" in this song.

Math
While the class performs this song, select a few students to count the number of seconds the performance takes. Record the times. Are they the same or different? Why? Repeat process with different counters.

Social Studies
Echoing or mirroring, a common way to learn, is used in this song. Name other activities that use echoing or mirroring.

Science
Discuss the concept of sound and echoes (sound waves, vibrations). How are echoes produced?

Art
Draw a symmetrical picture. The picture on one half of the page is mirrored exactly on the other half of the page.

13. FIND A PARTNER

Words and Music by BRAD GREEN

(2-measure introduction on recording)

In a country style (♩ = 88)

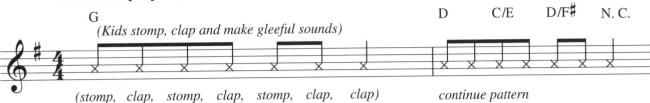

(Kids stomp, clap and make gleeful sounds)

G   D   C/E   D/F♯   N. C.

(stomp, clap, stomp, clap, stomp, clap, clap)   *continue pattern*

G

1. When it's your turn, find   a part - ner.
2. you're a - lone with - out   a part - ner,

D

Stand   by the per - son next to you.
Some - one else   is with - out one too.

G

Side - by - side when you find   a part - ner;
Raise your hand so   they can see it.

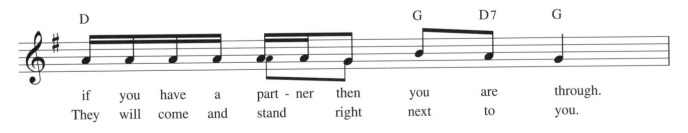

D   G   D7   G

if you have a part - ner then you are through.
They will come and stand right next to you.

1.   G/D D7 G *(sing)*   2.   C   G/D D7 G

(stomp, clap, stomp, clap, stomp, clap, clap) If   *(stomp, clap, stomp, clap, stomp, clap, clap)*

Teacher Tips

When to Use the Song
Finding a partner—a common event— should not be embarrassing or frightening for children. This song contains the full procedure. If there are an odd number of students, choose to either have the teacher participate, or have one group with three students.

Rule/Procedure
Finding a partner

Similar Songs
#1   Always Share

#5   Buenos Dias

#12 Everybody Listen

#16 Give Me the Magic Five!

#24 Life Is Better With a Friend

#26 Make a Circle

#27 Make a Line

#28 Marshmallow Mouth

#34 Show Respect

Musical Activities
- Begin with the pat-clap pattern and then start singing when desired.
- Have students create 4-beat patterns of pats, claps, or snaps to perform during the parts of the song where there is no singing (measures 1–4, 6, 8, 10, 12).

Movement Activities
Hold a contest to see how quickly and quietly students can find a partner.

Cross-Curricular Activities
Reading/Language Arts
- Discuss and practice syllable division. Have students identify all the one-syllable and two-syllable words in this song.
- Have students practice reading to a partner— an important technique for emerging readers.

Writing
Encourage students to write a story with a partner and share it with the class.

Math
Working with a partner, have students create a math problem based on the skills currently being studied. Switch and solve each other's problem. Check for accuracy.

Social Studies
Make a list of things that you do that requires a partner (lifting large objects, partner dancing, playing catch, for example).

Science
Introduce the concept of magnets. Explore how a magnet is always searching for its partner, or polar opposite.

14. FOLLOW THE INSTRUCTIONS

(4-measure introduction on recording)

Words and Music by BRAD GREEN

Copyright © 2009 by HAL LEONARD CORPORATION
International Copyright Secured   All Rights Reserved

The original purchaser of this book has permission to reproduce this song for educational use in one school only. Any other use is strictly prohibited.

Teacher Tips

When to Use the Song
Following instructions is a life-long skill. Sing this song with students before giving detailed or important instructions to direct and focus listening.

Rule/Procedure
Listening closely to instructions

Brief Version
Sing measures 1–4 and 13–16 (with the pick-up notes).

Similar Songs
#6   Clap One Time If You Can Hear My Voice

#12   Everybody Listen

#20   Hocus Pocus, Everybody Focus

#46   You'll Need Your *(Book)* for This Activity

Musical Activities
- Sing this song as a call and response. After the students know the song well, have different student volunteers be the leaders.

- Divide class into three groups. Assign each group one note from the first measure— D, F-sharp, or A. Sing and sustain the assigned notes to form a chord. The teacher then sings the song while the students sustain the chord. Have students identify when the chord sounds good with the melody and not. This helps to develop part-singing, listening and harmonic skills.

Cross-Curricular Activities
Reading/Language Arts
Identify and define words that provide order to instructions such as numbering or sequence words (first, second, next, after, before, and so forth).

Writing
Write a numbered list of instructions (how to bake a cake, brush your teeth, for example).

Math
Instructions and order are essential in math. Make a list of things that require order or sequence in math (counting by 1's, 2's, 5's, least to greatest, and so forth).

Social Studies
Identify events or activities in the school or family that require following instructions.

Science
Design instructions, in the proper order, to carry out an age appropriate science experiment.

15. GET READY TO START THE DAY

(4-measure introduction on recording)

Words and Music by BRAD GREEN

* Substitute with other words, as needed.

 Teacher Tips

When to Use the Song
- Sing this song as a greeting at the beginning of the day, and when you are ready to begin a new activity.
- Alternate uses: 1) Replace the word "book" with any supplies or materials that are needed. 2) Repeat the middle section until all the needed materials have been named.

Rule/Procedure
Focusing, starting the day, greeting

Brief Version
Sing measures 1–8 (with pick-up note) and measures 13–20.

Similar Songs
#5   Buenos Dias

#10   Do You Have What You Need?

#19   Hello

#46   You'll Need Your (Book) for This Activity

Musical Activities
- Perform as a call and response. After the students know the song well, have student volunteers serve as the leaders.
- Divide the class into four groups. Assign each group one note from the opening measures—middle C, E, G, C. Sing and sustain the assigned notes to form a chord. Singing chords will help students develop part-singing skills.
- Use the rhythm of the first full measure as a repeating rhythmic pattern, or *ostinato*. Have students perform this pattern by clapping or playing rhythm instruments while singing the song.

Cross-Curricular Activities

Writing
Have a contest to see who can list the most rhyming words with the word "day."

Math
This song is about the things that we need to start the school day. What elements are necessary to work math problems? *(an equation, a problem to solve, numbers, and so forth)*.

Social Studies
Discuss the things you need to start your day. *(what you have for breakfast, what you need to wear, what to put in your backpack, and so forth)*

Art
Make a list of the materials needed to complete an assigned art project.

Physical Education/Health
Have the class make a list of things people do every morning to stay healthy.

16. GIVE ME THE MAGIC FIVE!

(2-measure introduction on recording)

2-Beat (♩ = 120)

Words and Music by BRAD GREEN

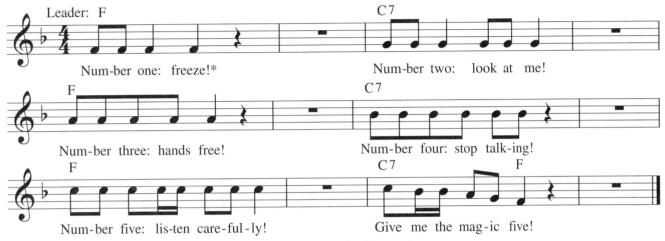

Leader: F
Num-ber one: freeze!*

C7
Num-ber two: look at me!

F
Num-ber three: hands free!

C7
Num-ber four: stop talk-ing!

F
Num-ber five: lis-ten care-ful-ly!

C7   F
Give me the mag-ic five!

* Wait for the students to follow each instruction before continuing to sing.

 Teacher Tips

When to Use the Song

This activity is used to get student attention in a very short amount of time. When first learning the procedure, sing the song while raising the fingers of the hand. After the students have memorized and practiced the procedure, it is only necessary to raise the fingers without singing the song.

Rule/Procedure

Coming to attention or quieting the students quickly

Similar Songs

\# 8   Come to Attention

\#12   Everybody Listen

\#20   Hocus Pocus, Everybody Focus

\#32   Rules Song

Musical Activities

- Study melodic contour. When does the melody move up, down, or stay the same?
- After the song is learned, have students play it on melodic instruments.

- Discover the range in this song by having students raise their hands when they sing the highest pitch, and touch the floor when they sing the lowest pitch. *(C, F)*

Cross-Curricular Activities

Reading/Language Arts
Present the concept of the exclamation point. How is one used in this song?

Writing
Write a sentence that ends with an exclamation point.

Math
Make a list of things that come in sets of five. *(fingers/toes, gum, counting by fives)*

Social Studies
This activity song communicates instructions first through singing, then with a silent hand motion. Discuss other non-verbal ways that people communicate with each other.

Science
Study a barred instrument such as a xylophone, and discover what physical changes occur with the bars as the pitch goes higher or lower.

17. GO BACK TO YOUR PLACE

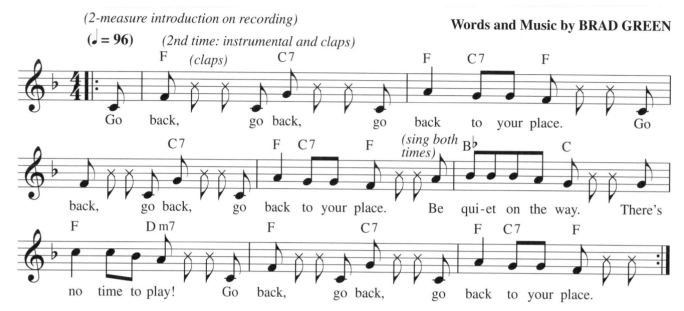

(2-measure introduction on recording)

($\downarrow$ = 96)   (2nd time: instrumental and claps)

Words and Music by BRAD GREEN

Go back, go back, go back to your place. Go back, go back, go back to your place. Be qui-et on the way. There's no time to play! Go back, go back, go back to your place.

 **Teacher Tips**

When to Use the Song
To help students stay quiet and focused as they move back to their places.

Rule/Procedure
Going back to your place quietly

Similar Songs
#6   Clap One Time If You Can Hear My Voice
#12   Everybody Listen
#16   Give Me the Magic Five!
#26   Make a Circle
#27   Make a Line
#28   Marshmallow Mouth
#29   Move in 5-4-3-2-1
#36   Stand Up/Sit Down
#41   Walk, Don't Run!
#43   When You Need to Move Around the Room

Musical Activities
• Compare the pitches F, G, A on the word "back" in the opening measures to the pitches A, G, F in the last measure.

• Perform the rhythm of the words on a percussion instrument, and the hand claps on a contrasting percussion instrument.

Movement Activities
Substitute the hand claps with a snap, stomp, pat, or tap.

Cross-Curricular Activities

Reading/Language Arts
The word "back" has two meanings: 1) a part of the body, or 2) something in the past. List other words that have more than one meaning.

Writing
Have students write a short story about a time when they went to the wrong place. What was the result?

Math
Have students count the number of times they sing the word "back."

Social Studies
List places where it is important for one to stay in his/her place. *(in an airplane, in a car, in a dentist's chair, for example)*

18. THE GOLDEN RULE

(4-measure introduction on recording)

Words and Music by BRAD GREEN

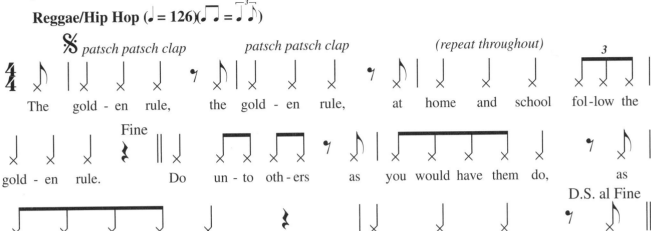

Copyright © 2009 by HAL LEONARD CORPORATION
International Copyright Secured   All Rights Reserved

 **Teacher Tips**

When to Use the Song
Use this song to teach the Golden Rule, one of the most important rules in life.

Rule/Procedure
Treating others with respect

Similar Songs
#18   The Golden Rule
#34   Show Respect
#38   Take Turns
#44   When You Say "Hello"
#45   When You Use Good Manners

Musical Activities
- Have students perform a 4-beat pattern: pat, pat, clap, rest. Teacher chants the speech chorus while students continue the pattern. Repeat until students learn the chant.
- Have students improvise complimentary rhythms on percussion instruments using the rhythm of the song as a starting point.

Cross-Curricular Activities

Reading/Language Arts
Have students read *The Berenstain Bears and the Golden Rule* by Stan Berenstain.

Writing
Present a famous proverb. Have students write a paragraph about its meaning. ("Many hands make light work." "Practice makes perfect." "Two heads are better than one.")

Math
Measure different items in the room with a ruler. Measure length, width, and depth.

Science
Describe ways that the Golden Rule could be applied in a science lab. For example, be organized with materials so that they are ready for others to use when you have finished.

Social Studies
List places in school or the community where people must cooperate with each other to function properly. *(driving in traffic, waiting in line, obeying the laws, and so forth)*

Art
Draw an illustration that demonstrates the meaning of the Golden Rule.

19. HELLO

(2-measure introduction on recording)

Words and Music by BRAD GREEN

Relaxed 2-beat (♩ = 100)

Leader: C   Echo: G7

Hel - lo!   (Hel-lo!)   How   are   you?   (How   are   you?)   It's

C

so   good   (it's   so   good)   to   see   you.   (to   see   you.)   I'm

F

glad   you're   here   to - day.   (I'm   glad   you're   here   to - day.)   Let's

C

have   some   fun,   O.   K?   (Let's   have   some   fun,   O.   K?)   We'll

F   G   C   F   G   C

sing   and   dance   and   play,   (We'll   sing   and   dance   and   play,)   and

G7   C   G7   C

then   go   on   our   way.   (and   then   go   on   our   way.)

 Teacher Tips

When to Use the Song
Letting students know that the teacher is glad they are present helps to create a warm, learning environment. Use this greeting with students as they enter the room, to begin a lesson, or to start the day.

Rule/Procedure
As a greeting, to welcome students to school or class

Brief Version
Sing the first four measures only.

Similar Songs
#5   Buenos Dias

#22 It's Time To Say Goodbye

#30 Please and Thank You

#44 When You Say "Hello"

#45 When You Use Good Manners

Musical Activities
- A beautiful way to encourage individual singing is with a pretend microphone. The teacher holds the microphone to mouth during the call and extends it to individual students for the response. Make sure all students have the opportunity to sing.

- Play the rhythm of the words on rhythm instruments.

Movement Activities
Substitute the words with different body percussion sounds (clap, stomp, snap, tap).

Cross-Curricular Activities

Reading/Language Arts
List different words and phrases that are used for greeting one another.

Writing
- Identify the rhyming words in this song. Create a new list of rhyming words, and then have students write *verse*, or a poem with a fixed rhyme scheme or meter.

- Practice writing dialogue using the phrases in this song.

Math
Have students count the number of words in each echo. Determine which echoes have the same number of words.

Social Studies
Learn to say "Hello" in other languages.

20. HOCUS POCUS, EVERYBODY FOCUS

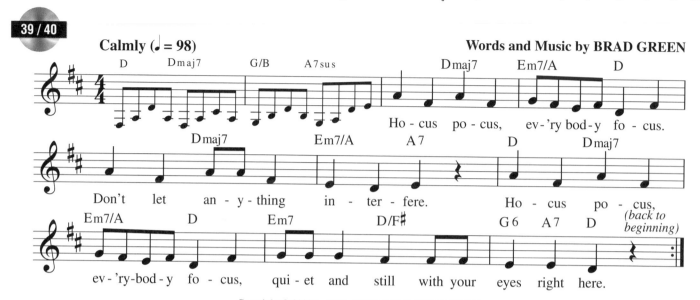

Calmly (♩ = 98)

Words and Music by BRAD GREEN

Teacher Tips

When to Use the Song
Insert this song in the middle of teaching when attention is waning.

Rule/Procedure
Focusing attention; reminding students to concentrate; practicing listening skills

Similar Songs
#6   Clap One Time If You Can Hear My Voice

#8   Come to Attention

#16   Give Me the Magic Five!

#32   Rules Song

Musical Activities
- Determine the form. Teacher sings each two-measure phrase and students echo. Then, lead students to determine which phrases are the same and which ones are different. Label the first phrase "a." Sing the second phrase (children echo). The same or different? (*different*). Label that phrase "b." Sing third phrase. Same or different? (*same as first phrase*). Label third phrase "a." Sing final phrase. (*different from the others*). Label the last phrase "c." Form of the song is abac.

- Have students compose a melody on barred instruments in abac form. Make each phrase the same length, and end on *do*.

Cross-Curricular Activities

Reading/Language Arts
A magician often says "hocus-pocus" when performing a trick to grab the audience's attention. Make a list of words or phrases that are used to help us focus our attention.

Math
Perform a math trick: The Number Three Trick. (1) Take a number. (2) Double it. (3) Add nine. (4) Subtract three. (5) Divide by two. (6) Subtract your original number. (7) Your answer should be three. Find other math tricks for students to enjoy.

Science
Perform a science trick (like a magician).
Action: Magician presents a cup full of water with pepper sprinkled across the top. A volunteer puts index finger in water. Nothing happens. The magician puts index finger in the water and the pepper separates to the edges of the cup.
Secret: Before the trick, rub soap on your index finger (this will separate the pepper). MAGIC!

21. IT'S OK TO HAVE DIFFERENT FEELINGS

(4-measure introduction on recording)

Words and Music by BRAD GREEN

41 / 42

Confident energy! (♩ = 128)

You are be - ing a hu - man be - ing,

when you're feel - ing dif - f'rent feel - ings.

If you're cry - ing, or you're laugh - ing,

it's O. K. to have dif - f'rent feel - ings.

Some - times we get mad. Some - times we are glad.

Some - times we make noise, *(yell!)* but oth - er times qui - et is what we en - joy!

CODA

It's O. K. to have dif - f'rent feel - ings.

Teacher Tips

When to Use the Song
- Use this song to help students feel comfortable about expressing emotions; for example, when they are embarrassed about crying, or how to manage anger.
- Understanding and expressing different emotions in a healthy way is an important part of being a good citizen.

Rule/Procedure
Managing emotions; self-esteem

Similar Songs
#18   The Golden Rule

#24   Life Is Better With a Friend

Musical Activities
- When performing this song, use expressive singing to convey the different feelings such as crying, laughing, mad, glad, loud or quiet. Ask students to identify the expressive qualities they used to portray each feeling.
- Have students determine the highest and lowest pitches in this song. *(highest – B; lowest – D)*

Cross-Curricular Activities
Reading/Language Arts
Make a list of nouns and verbs that describe a single emotion.

Writing
Have students compose a story about a person who is feeling one of the emotions described in this song. Ask volunteers to share their stories.

Math
Create a bar graph based on a class survey of emotions felt. Begin by listing three common emotions. Students survey classmates/friends on which of the three emotions were felt that day; then, draw a bar graph with each bar representing the frequency of an emotion surveyed.

Social Studies
Guide students in a game of emotion charades: Have students pantomime an emotion or feeling. The student who correctly guesses the emotion gets the next turn.

Science
Research and find ways that emotions can influence one's physical health. In what ways can exercise and other activities improve one's emotional health?

Art
Have students create a picture that represents a chosen emotion or feeling.

22. IT'S TIME TO SAY GOODBYE

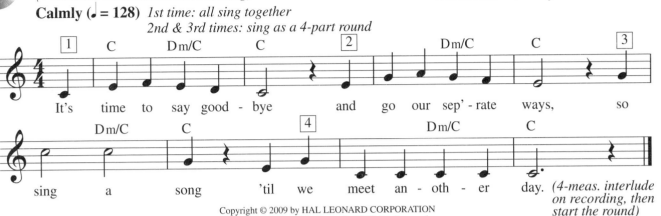

Teacher Tips

When to Use the Song
Use this song as a beautiful and soothing ending to a lesson, or class period.

Rule/Procedure
To be used when ending the school day or a lesson

Similar Songs
#5   Buenos Dias

#19   Hello

#30   Please and Thank You

#40   Toodle-Oodle-Oo

#44   When You Say "Hello"

#45   When You Use Good Manners

Musical Activities
- Use this song to practice beautiful *legato* phrasing and to develop part-singing skills. May be performed as a 2-, 3-, or 4-part canon.
- Have students play the song for memory on barred instruments.

Cross-Curricular Activities

Reading/Language Arts
Have students identify the rhyming words in this song.

Writing
Have students write as many different ways to say "goodbye" as they can in an allotted amount of time.

Math
Telling time. Have students record the various times throughout the day that they say "goodbye" to family members, teachers, and friends. Demonstrate the times on a clock.

Social Studies
Learn to say "goodbye" in other languages.

Science
Experiment: Say Goodbye to Water.

Fill several containers with water and place them in different parts of the room (in the sunlight, in a dark corner, near a heater vent). Measure and record the water levels weekly for one month. Discover the fastest rate of evaporation, or discover which container says "goodbye" to the water the fastest. Explain why.

Art
Have students create a comic strip in which the characters say goodbye to one another. Plan the strip and write the captions before drawing the illustrations.

23. KEEP YOUR HANDS TO YOURSELF

(4-measure introduction on recording)

Words and Music by BRAD GREEN

Moderate Calypso (♩ = 132)

Keep your hands to your-self where they be - long.— Be - ing im - po - lite— is al - ways wrong. So ev - 'ry - one— can get a - long, — keep your hands to your-self where they be - long.—

 Teacher Tips

When to Use the Song

Use this song to remind students of good behavior; specifically, keeping their hands to themselves.

Rule/Procedure

Managing emotions; respecting others; keeping your hands to yourself

Similar Songs

#18   The Golden Rule

#27   Make a Line

#34   Show Respect

#43   When You Need to Move Around the Room

#45   When You Use Good Manners

Musical Activities

• Add rhythm instruments such as wood blocks, claves, guiro, triangles, and drums.

• Listen to other forms of calypso music, including steel drum bands.

Cross-Curricular Activities

Reading/Language Arts
Share a famous story from Greek mythology about touching—*Midas and the Midas Touch.*

Writing
Make a list of different ways that people communicate nonverbally with their hands. Have students write a description of one of these forms of communication.

Social Studies
This song is written in calypso style, a type of music that originated in the Caribbean Islands. Locate the Caribbean Islands on a map.

Science
Calypso style music can be heard in the Caribbean Islands. Examine the ocean animals of the Caribbean islands region.

Art
Make a Caribbean art project with seashells.

Physical Education
With a focus on team sports, review safety factors/rules/situations that require players to keep their hands to themselves.

24. LIFE IS BETTER WITH A FRIEND

(4-measure introduction on recording)

Words and Music by BRAD GREEN

1st time: All sing Part 1
2nd time: All sing Part 2
3rd time: Sing parts together

Teacher Tips

When to Use the Song

- Sing this song when children need to be reminded that we should be kind because we all need friends.

- This song can be used to celebrate friendship and to remember the importance of making friends.

Rule/Procedure

Making friends

Similar Songs

#13   Find A Partner

#18   The Golden Rule

#34   Show Respect

#44   When You Say "Hello"

Musical Activities

After students know the song very well, divide them into two groups. Have one group perform the ostinato section, while the other group sings the melody.

Cross-Curricular Activities

Reading/Language Arts

As a vocabulary lesson, make a list of synonyms for the word "friends."

Writing

Write a poem about friends or friendship.

Math

Demonstrate multiplication by showing how many friendly acts would result if two people passed on a friendly act to two other people, then three other people.

Social Studies

Encourage students to practice being friendly. Make a list of behaviors or actions that show friendliness towards others.

Science

Study animal behavior by discussing how an animal or pet can be a friend.

Art

Help students make a piece of art dedicated to friendship. Create an illustration to accompany the poetry written in the Writing assignment.

25. MAKE A CHOICE

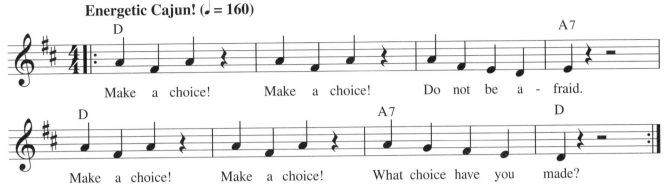

(4-measure introduction on recording)

Words and Music by BRAD GREEN

Energetic Cajun! (♩ = 160)

Make a choice! Make a choice! Do not be a-fraid.

Make a choice! Make a choice! What choice have you made?

 Teacher Tips

When to Use the Song
Many activities require students to make a choice, and this can be difficult for some, and may become time consuming. Use this song when encouraging students to make a choice.

Rule/Procedure
Decision-making

Similar Songs
#13 Find a Partner

#31 Polka Dot Spot

Musical Activities
- Give students the opportunity to individually sing and/or play on a barred instrument the three notes found in measures 1, 2, 5, and 6 (A, F-sharp, A). Is the motive "make a choice" the same every time it is presented? *(yes)*
- Determine the form of this song. *(abac)*

Cross-Curricular Activities

Reading/Language Arts
Guide students to practice making choices about creating words. Give students a bag of magnet letters, and have each student choose one letter. Based on that letter, let students choose a word containing that letter.

Writing
Write a story about a person who had to make a choice and then, develop how the person dealt with the consequences of that choice.

Math
For older students: Discover probability.

Gather several red, green, yellow, purple and blue pieces of candy or crayons. Place the items in a bag. Teach students how to determine the probability that they will pull out a certain color. Calculate this by counting the total number of items in the bag. Count the number of red items in the bag (for example). Divide the number of red items by the total number of items. The result is the percentage probability that a person will pull out a red item.

Social Studies
Keep a journal for one day and document the choices made throughout the day. (What to wear to school, what to eat at lunch, what to watch on TV, and so forth). Are students surprised at the number of choices we make each day?

Science
What choices can we make to recycle materials and help the environment for the future?

Physical Education/Health
Make a list of healthy choices to make when choosing snacks and lunch items.

26. MAKE A CIRCLE

(8-measure introduction on recording)

Words and Music by BRAD GREEN

With a light bounce (♩. = 84)

Cir - cle, cir - cle, make a cir - cle. Make it nice and

round. Cir - cle, cir - cle, make a cir - cle.

Don't make a sound. Cir - cle, cir - cle,

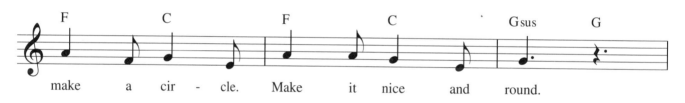

make a cir - cle. Make it nice and round.

Cir - cle, cir - cle, make a cir - cle. Now sit down.

Copyright © 2009 by HAL LEONARD CORPORATION
International Copyright Secured   All Rights Reserved

The original purchaser of this book has permission to reproduce this song for educational use in one school only. Any other use is strictly prohibited.

Teacher Tips

When to Use the Song
Many games and activities require students to make a circle. Have the students sing this song while they move into a circle to save time and remove opportunity for talking.

Rule/Procedure
Making a circle

Brief Version
Sing the first four and the last four measures.

Similar Songs
#13 Find a Partner

#14 Follow the Instructions

#16 Give Me the Magic Five!

#17 Go Back To Your Place

#23 Keep Your Hands to Yourself

#29 Move in 5-4-3-2-1

#31 Polka Dot Spot

#36 Stand Up/Sit Down

#37 Stay In Your Seat

Musical Activities
• The meter in this song is 6/8, which gives it a lilting, skipping feel. Sing/chant other songs/rhymes in 6/8 meter such as "Humpty Dumpty," "Jack and Jill," "Row, Row, Row Your Boat" and so forth.

Cross-Curricular Activities
Reading/Language Arts
When printing, identify and draw the letters that have circles or circular shapes in them.

Writing
Write a fictional story about a ball and its many adventures.

Math
Have students divide a circle into 2 equal parts; 3 equal parts; 4 equal parts.

Social Studies
Introduce the globe, a circular orb that represents the earth. Have students locate their country and state on the globe. Locate other places of interest.

Science
Conduct experiments with a ping-pong ball and an incline. Using the same sized board for the incline, have students time how long it takes the ball to travel down the board when the incline is low, medium, and very steep.

Art
Create a piece of artwork that uses circles of various sizes, and that overlap with one another. Color or paint the final piece.

Physical Education
Make a list of games that are played in a circle or use a round ball.

27. MAKE A LINE

(4-measure introduction on recording)

Words and Music by BRAD GREEN

With friendliness ($\quad$ = 104)

One and two, class is through; three and four, walk to the door.

Num-ber five, hands at your side; be ver-y still when you ar-rive.

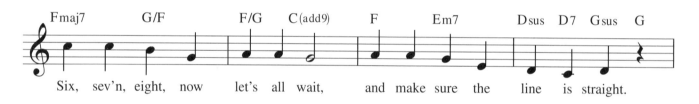

Six, sev'n, eight, now let's all wait, and make sure the line is straight.

Num-ber nine, a per-fect line. Num-ber ten, I'll see you a-gain.

Teacher Tips

When to Use the Song
When students need to form a line

Rule/Procedure
Making a line

Similar Songs
#14   Follow the Instructions

#16   Give Me the Magic Five!

#17   Go Back to Your Place

#23   Keep Your Hands to Yourself

#29   Move in 5-4-3-2-1

#36   Stand Up/ Sit Down

Musical Activities
- Have students show with their hands the direction of the melody when singing the words "one and two," "class is through," "three and four," "Number five," "at your side," "very still," "Number nine," "perfect line." *(upward)* Have them show the direction of the melody when singing the words "you arrive" and "you again." *(downward)*

- Sing the entire song and show the melodic contour of the melody with the rise and fall of the hands.

Cross-Curricular Activities
Reading/Language Arts
Read children's books that deal with counting to ten.

Writing
Draw a straight line on the board. Ask students to finish this story, "Once upon a time there was a line…"

Math
Draw lines of different sizes and then practice measuring the lines with a ruler.

Social Studies
Make a list of places where people stand in lines. Why do we stand in line?

Science
Using mirrors and objects large enough to cast shadows, help students discover that light travels in straight lines.

Art
Have students draw straight lines with a ruler to form a variety of shapes.

Physical Education
Make a list of games that are played in a line formation.

28. MARSHMALLOW MOUTH

(4-measure introduction on recording)

Words and Music by BRAD GREEN

Funky! (♩ = 132)

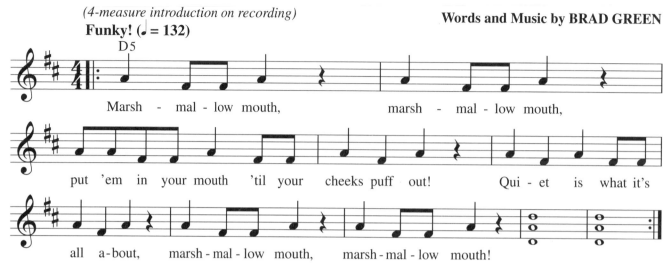

Have students place a large imaginary marshmallow in their mouth after this song.

 Teacher Tips

When to Use the Song
This song gives students something to do and visualize while they are quiet.

Rule/Procedure
Staying quiet

Brief version
Sing the first four measures only.

Similar Songs
#12   Everybody Listen
#16   Give Me the Magic Five!
#32   Rules Song
#34   Show Respect
#38   Take Turns
#45   When You Use Good Manners

Musical Activities
- Have students play this song on a prepared barred instrument with all bars removed except A and F-sharp. Label A as "high" and F-sharp as "low."

- Sing the song while pretending that the mouth is full of marshmallows. Describe the results. Discuss the importance of good diction when singing.

Cross-Curricular Activities

Reading/Language Arts
Have students read a passage aloud in two different ways: once as if they had a mouthful of marshmallows, and again using good diction.

Math
Name three other items that are cylindrical in shape.

Social Studies
Have students make a list of places where they need to use their "marshmallow mouths," or be very quiet. *(visiting someone in the hospital, library, when baby is sleeping, when someone else is talking)*

Art
Use marshmallow and glue to create a sculpture.

Physical Education
Play a relay game in which the children must walk across the room and back, carrying a marshmallow on a spoon, without dropping the marshmallow.

29. MOVE IN 5-4-3-2-1

(4-measure introduction on recording)

Words and Music by BRAD GREEN

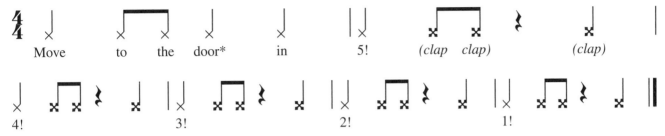

Energetically (♩ = 144)

Move   to   the   door*   in   5!   (clap   clap)   (clap)

4!   3!   2!   1!

* substitute as needed

Teacher Tips

When to Use the Song
When students are given a specific amount of time to move from one activity to the next, they tend to talk less, focus more, and less time is wasted. Use this chant when students need to move quickly from one area to the next.

Rule/Procedure
Quickly moving from one area to the next

Similar Songs
#6   Clap One Time If You Can Hear My Voice
#12   Everybody Listen
#14   Follow the Instructions
#16   Give Me the Magic Five!
#17   Go Back to Your Place
#23   Keep Your Hands to Yourself
#26   Make a Circle
#27   Make a Line
#28   Marshmallow Mouth
#36   Stand Up/Sit Down
#41   Walk, Don't Run!
#43   When You Need To Move Around the Room

Musical Activities
Fill in the blank with the words that are needed, such as "door," "circle," "line," "wall," and so forth.

Cross-Curricular Activities

Reading/Language Arts
Read children's books that deal with counting, a countdown, or the number 5.

Writing
Write a story that contains a 5-4-3-2-1 countdown.

Math
A countdown is a series of numbers. Explore other series of numbers such as counting by 2s or 5s or 10s.

Social Studies
Discuss with students about times when they need to move quickly. *(fire drill, to get help when someone is hurt, for example)*

Science
Use this song for students to get into position for science experiment quickly.

Physical Education
Have a contest to see how many (jumping jacks, jump rope, and so forth) that students can do in a specified amount of time.

30. PLEASE AND THANK YOU

(4-measure introduction on recording)

Words and Music by BRAD GREEN

Calmly (♩ = 126)

1st time: all sing together
2nd & 3rd times: sing as a 4-part round

We all say "please." We all say "thank you."
We are all po - lite. We are ve - ry kind.

Copyright © 2009 by HAL LEONARD CORPORATION
International Copyright Secured   All Rights Reserved

 Teacher Tips

When to Use the Song
"Please" and "thank you" are some of the most important words in the English language. Use this song to teach that we must use these words to be polite and kind to one another.

Rule/Procedure
Being polite

Similar Songs
#5   Buenos Dias
#19   Hello
#22   It's Time to Say Goodbye
#24   Life Is Better With a Friend
#44   When You Say "Hello"
#45   When You Use Good Manners

Musical Activities
• Sing this song as a 2-, 3-, or 4-part round. Begin part-singing after the students have memorized the song. As the students sing, teacher sings the round. Then repeat the process, adding a few student singers to the teacher part. Finally, divide the group into two equal parts and sing as a round. At a later time, sing as a 3- or 4-part round.

• Each phrase uses the vowel sound "ah" in the word "all." How is proper singing different from speaking?

Cross-Curricular Activities

Reading/Language Arts
Have students read or read to the class Richard Scarry's *Please and Thank You Book.*

Writing
Have students think of a time when they used the word "please," and use that situation as a starting point for writing.

Math
Present a word problem using multiplication: "If two groups sing this song, and there were five in each group, how many total students would be singing?" Change the numbers to vary the problem.

Social Studies
Learn how to say "please" and "thank you" in other languages.

Physical Education
Play "Simon Says" with students following Simon's instructions only when Simon says "please."

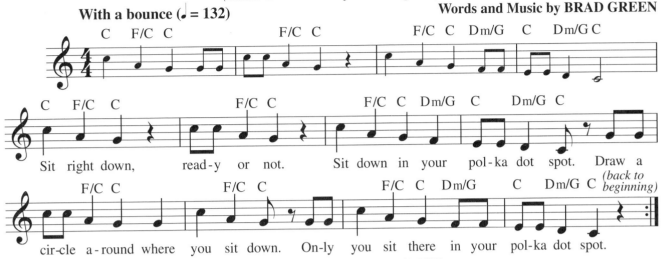

31. POLKA DOT SPOT

(thanks to Doris Music for this song idea)

Words and Music by BRAD GREEN

With a bounce (♩ = 132)

Sit right down, read-y or not. Sit down in your pol-ka dot spot. Draw a *(back to beginning)* cir-cle a-round where you sit down. On-ly you sit there in your pol-ka dot spot.

 Teacher Tips

When to Use the Song
This is a great visual to help young students understand how to sit in their own space.

Brief Version
Sing measures seven and eight only, "Sit down in your polka dot spot."

Rule/Procedure
Sitting and staying in your place

Similar Songs
#6   Clap One Time If You Can Hear My Voice

#12   Everybody Listen

#16   Give Me the Magic Five!

#23   Keep Your Hands to Yourself

#27   Make a Line

#36   Stand Up/Sit Down

#43   When You Need to Move Around the Room

Musical Activities
- Sing this song *staccato* throughout. Discuss the difference between *staccato* and *legato* singing. Then, practice singing the song both ways.

- Find the two phrases in the song with the words "polka dot spot." Determine the pitches to be *mi, re, do*. Have students sing the song again and play these two phrases as an *ostinato* on barred instruments using the notes E, D, and C.

Cross-Curricular Activities

Writing
Have students write an original story about an animal that has spots.

Math
Have students measure the distance between two spots.

Social Studies
Using a globe, help students find spots of importance such as 1) the United States, 2) Mexico, 3) the Atlantic and Pacific Oceans, 4) the Equator, 5) other.

Science
What animals have spots?

Art
Paint a picture with dots, using a cotton swab as a paintbrush and spots as brush strokes similar to "pointillism" style of painting.

Physical Education
Play a game with a Frisbee called "Hit the Spot." Two teams throw a Frisbee to hit a spot. Each team is awarded one point for each hit.

32. RULES SONG

(4-measure introduction on recording)
1st time: all sing together
2nd & 3rd times: sing as a 4-part round

Words and Music by BRAD GREEN

Calmly (♩ = 108)

Be po-lite to ev'ry-one. Raise your hand be-fore you speak.

Al - ways par-tic-i-pate. Make this room a learn - ing space.

 Teacher Tips

When to Use the Song
These are common rules that may be sung to remind students of appropriate classroom behavior.

Rule/Procedure
Politeness; raising your hand before speaking; participation; maintaining a learning environment

Similar Songs
#14 Follow the Instructions
#18 The Golden Rule
#34 Show Respect
#45 When You Use Good Manners

Musical Activities
• In a music class, substitute the words "learning space" for "singing space."
• Practice part-singing in two, three, or four parts by singing this song in a canon after the song has been memorized.

Cross-Curricular Activities
Reading/Language Arts
Practice vocabulary by having the students brainstorm words and phrases that describe a "learning place" or a "learning environment."

Writing
Write a descriptive paragraph: Use adjectives to describe an environment for learning such as a library or the classroom. Describe the people who are there, the size of the space, the furniture and all the other things in the room, and what action is taking place.

Math
As a class, make a list of math rules learned this year (this month or this week).

Social Studies
Discuss the importance of having rules at home; at school; in the community.

Science
Make a list of rules one should follow when visiting the animals at the zoo.

Physical Education
Learn the rules of a sport such as football, basketball, baseball, soccer, and so forth. Why are the rules needed?

33. SAY YOUR NAME

(2-measure introduction on recording)

Words and Music by BRAD GREEN

With attitude! (♩ = 132)

Say your name, ___ say your name. Say it loud ___ and

with no shame. Let's play a game, ___ and I'll ex - plain.

When you say your name, we'll say the same. ___ *cresc.* When you say your name, we'll

say the same. ___ When you say your name, we'll say the same!

GAME DIRECTIONS: Have children sit in a circle and keep a pat-clap-snap-snap rhythm while singing this song. At the end of the song, have a child speak his/her name on the next pat (strong beat.) The class repeats the name on the next pat (strong beat.)

 Teacher Tips

When to Use the Song
Use this song to help students learn the names of their classmates and to build community.

Rule/Procedure
Learning names

Similar Songs
#19 Hello
#24 Life Is Better With Friends
#44 When You Say "Hello"

Musical Activities
- As a variation, say every previous name (cumulative game) instead of only saying the name of one person.
- Accompany this song with various rhythm instruments.

Cross-Curricular Activities

Reading/Language Arts
Have the class determine the number of syllables in each student's first name. Make a chart with columns, and write the names with one syllable in one column, the names with two syllables in another column, and so forth.

Math
Calculate the number of names that would be said if everyone in class said his/her own name and one other person's name. *(number in class times two)*

Social Studies
Identify different ways that people who have important statements to make can have them heard by a large audience. *(microphones, mass media, TV, radio, Internet).*

Science
Investigate the ways that sound is amplified.

34. SHOW RESPECT

(4-measure introduction on recording)

Words and Music by BRAD GREEN

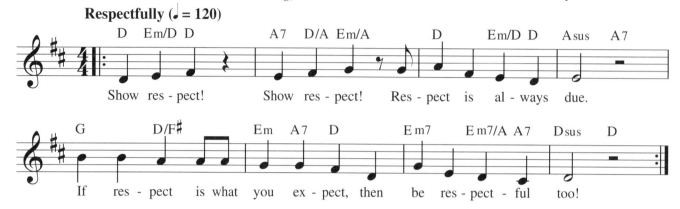

Teacher Tips

When to Use the Song
Becoming a respectful person is a goal for each individual, and this song helps us to remember to show respect.

Brief Version
Sing the first four measures.

Rule/Procedure
Being respectful

Similar Songs
#18 The Golden Rule

#24 Life Is Better With a Friend

#38 Take Turns

#44 When You Say "Hello"

#45 When You Use Good Manners

Musical Activities
When performing, add drums and cymbals to imitate a marching band.

Cross-Curricular Activities
Reading/Language Arts
Read the book *Respect and Take Care of Things (Learning to Get Along)* by Cheri J. Meiners.

Writing
Write a short article on three ways to show respect.

Math
Solve a word problem using inches and feet: "The flagpole in front of the school that holds the American flag is 10 feet tall. How many inches high is the flagpole?" *(12 inches x 10 = 120 inches)*

Social Studies
Make a list of the different ways that we show respect towards the American flag.

Science
Discuss why it is important to be careful and show respect when conducting a science experiment.

Art
Make a collage from newspapers and magazines that illustrates people showing respect in a variety of ways (to others, to the flag, to special things, to our parents, and so forth).

35. A SONG TO PASS THINGS OUT

(2-measure introduction on recording)

Words and Music by BRAD GREEN

Energetic 2-beat (♩ = 126)

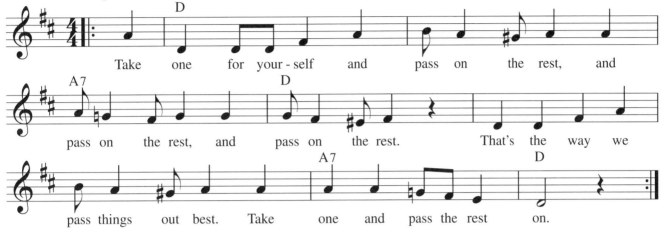

Take one for your-self and pass on the rest, and pass on the rest, and pass on the rest. That's the way we pass things out best. Take one and pass the rest on.

 Teacher Tips

When to Use the Song

Distributing things is one of the most frequent procedures in a classroom. An efficient way to distribute papers is to pass the entire stack and have students take one item from the top for themselves.

Brief Version

Sing the first line without the last "and."

Rule/Procedure

Distributing things

Related Songs

#1   Always Share

#7   Clean Up!

#10   Do You Have What You Need?

#37   Stay in Your Seat

#46   You'll Need Your *(Book)* for This Activity

Musical Activities

- Define a musical sequence. *(A series of musical phrases where a theme or melody is repeated, with some change each time, such as in pitch or length.)* Have students find the sequence in this song. *(measures 2, 3 and 4)*

- Use this song to pass out papers. Students pass the entire stack and take one item from the top for themselves. Teach them to pass the entire stack to the next student on the rest in measure 4 and again on the rest in measure 8.

Cross-Curricular Activities

Reading/Language Arts

This song is about "passing on the rest." What are some ways in conversation that we can politely indicate that we are finished speaking, and "pass" the conversation to the next person?

Writing

This song uses the word "best." Make a list of words that have degrees such as "good, better, and best" or "small, medium, large."

Math

Solve a word problem using multiplication: "If there are 500 sheets of paper in a ream and the teacher buys 3 reams of paper for the computer lab, how many sheets of paper did the teacher buy?" *(1500)*

Social Studies

Discuss the different ways that things are distributed in your community such as newspapers or the mail.

Science

Discover how paper is made. Visit a paper factory.

36. STAND UP / SIT DOWN

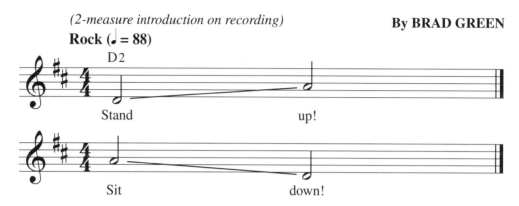

(2-measure introduction on recording)

Rock (♩ = 88)

By BRAD GREEN

D2

Stand   up!

Sit   down!

Use a hand gesture to accompany standing up or sitting down to make these directions more explicit.

 **Teacher Tips**

When to Use the Song
Use this song whenever the students need to quietly and quickly stand up or sit down.

Rule/Procedure
Standing up or sitting down

Similar Songs
#9   Criss-Cross Applesauce

#16   Give Me the Magic Five!

#26   Make a Circle

#27   Make a Line

#29   Move in 5-4-3-2-1

#37   Stay in Your Seat

Musical Activities
• Divide the class into two groups and let one group sustain the first note while the other group sings the second note. Tell the class that the distance between these two notes is a *fifth* because the two pitches (D and A) are five notes apart. *(do, re, mi, fa, sol).*

• Play the notes D and A (or *do* and *sol* in any key) on a barred instrument to accompany this and many other songs in this book.

Cross-Curricular Activities
Reading/Language Arts
Just as people stand up and sit down, letters can do the same when they are capitalized or lower case. Help students list the rules for capitalizing letters.

Writing
Encourage students to interview a friend about a time when they "stood up" or took a stand for something that they believed in. Share selected stories with the class.

Math
Create patterns with rectangular-shaped blocks that are on their side and standing up.

Social Studies
Share ways that people can stand up and make important statements, having them heard by a large audience.

Science
This song is about standing up and sitting down. In similar way, plants can grow up or creep along the ground. Investigate why plants grow in different ways.

37. STAY IN YOUR SEAT

(7-measure introduction on recording)

Words and Music by BRAD GREEN

Energetic party! (♩ = 102)

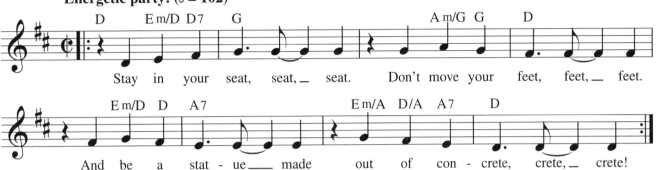

Stay in your seat, seat, __ seat. Don't move your feet, feet, __ feet.

And be a stat - ue __ made out of con - crete, crete, __ crete!

Teacher Tips

When to Use the Song
This song encourages students to follow the rule "stay in your seat" in a gentle way. The reminder asks them to occupy themselves by freezing like a statue.

Rule/Procedure
Remaining in your seat

Similar Songs
#17 Go Back to Your Place

#18 The Golden Rule

#27 Make a Line

#31 Polka Dot Spot

#34 Show Respect

#36 Stand Up/Sit Down

#43 When You Need to Move Around the Room

#45 When You Use Good Manners

Musical Activities
- Create a rhythmic clapping pattern to accompany this song.
- Add rhythm instruments such as wood blocks, claves, guiro, triangles, and drums.

- Practice making different statues. Model a high, medium, and low statue for the students. Play a recording, and when the music stops, have them freeze into their statues. At the next stop, they should become a different statue.

Cross-Curricular Activities

Reading/Language Arts
Read and spell correctly the three rhyming words in this song. *(seat, feet, concrete)*

Writing
Have students write an original story about a young person who is stuck in his/her chair and the adventures that follow.

Math
Randomly assign each student a number (one to the total number in class). Place tape on the floor in a snake-like formation. On a signal, have students quickly arrange themselves in number order according to the numbers they were assigned.

Social Studies
Name three famous statues and identify where they are located.

Science
Discuss how concrete is made and its many uses.

Art
Have students create a sculpture out of a compound that will harden.

38. TAKE TURNS

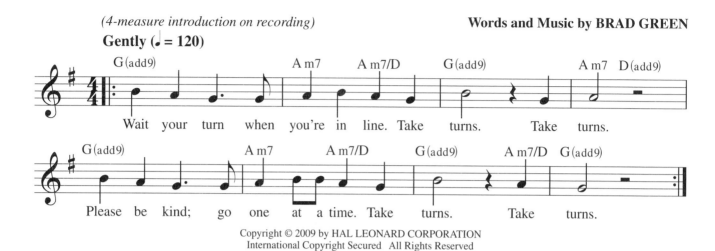

(4-measure introduction on recording)   **Words and Music by BRAD GREEN**

Gently (♩ = 120)

Wait your turn when you're in line. Take turns. Take turns.

Please be kind; go one at a time. Take turns. Take turns.

Copyright © 2009 by HAL LEONARD CORPORATION
International Copyright Secured   All Rights Reserved

The original purchaser of this book has permission to reproduce this song for educational use in one school only. Any other use is strictly prohibited.

 Teacher Tips

When to Use The Song
Use this song to teach the concept of taking turns, which is an important lesson of life.

Brief Version
Sing the last four measures.

Rule/Procedure
Taking turns; going one at a time

Similar Songs
#1   Always Share

#18   The Golden Rule

#25   Make a Choice

#34   Show Respect

#45   When You Use Good Manners

#46   You'll Need Your *(Book)* for This Activity

Musical Activities
• Have students create new statements about taking turns, such as "others like it when we take turns," or "taking turns saves time."

• Sing the song again inserting the new words in measures 1-2 and 5-6.

• Compare the two times the phrase "Take turns, take turns" appears. Are they the same or different? *(different)* Analyze the pitches for both. *(do-mi rest do-re* compared to *do-mi rest re-do).*

Cross-Curricular Activities
Reading/Language Arts
Review time-order words (first, next, then, after that, finally, for example). Follow a recipe that can be made in class, using these words.

Writing
Use the time-order words listed above to write directions from the classroom to the cafeteria or other locations in the building.

Math
Working in partners, have students take turns role-playing teacher/student. One student creates a math problem (teacher) and the other solves the problem (student). Reverse roles and do again.

Social Studies
Have students brainstorm about situations at home or at school where it is necessary to take turns.

Science
Discuss the importance of taking turns in science class when doing such things as looking into the microscope, observing items on display, or sharing special equipment.

39. THERE ARE TWO MINUTES LEFT

Words and Music by BRAD GREEN

There are two* min-utes left. May I sug-gest, watch the time and fin-ish the rest.

* substitute as needed

Teacher Tips

When to Use the Song
Use this song during timed activities such as writing, tests, individual or group work.

Rule/Procedure
Finishing on time

Similar Songs
#6   Clap One Time If You Can Hear My Voice

#8   Come to Attention

#22   It's Time to Say Goodbye

#37   Stay in Your Seat

Musical Activities
- Have students discover the two pitches in this song *(mi, sol)*, and then perform the song on a barred or keyboard instrument.
- Have students clap the rhythm of the words in the first four measures, and then the last four measures. Are the two phrases the same or different?

Cross-Curricular Activities

Reading/Language Arts
In a limited amount of time, have students list two words that start with the letters "A," "B," "C," and so forth.

Writing
Practice timed writing activities by giving students an allotted amount of time to write on a certain topic.

Math
Give a timed test to complete a set number of problems.

Social Studies
Discuss activities or events during the day that require one to watch the time. *(bedtime, catching the bus, school start and end time, sports practice, lessons, homework, and so forth)*

Science
Different liquids take a different amount of time to evaporate. Pour different liquids into individual cups and compare the time it takes for each of them to evaporate.

Physical Education
Have students time each other while running a certain distance.

40. TOODLE-OODLE-OO

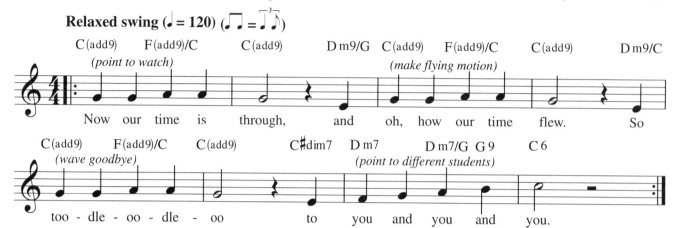

(2-measure introduction on recording)

Words and Music by BRAD GREEN

Now our time is through, and oh, how our time flew. So too-dle-oo-dle-oo to you and you and you.

(point to watch)

(make flying motion)

(wave goodbye)

(point to different students)

Copyright © 2009 by HAL LEONARD CORPORATION
International Copyright Secured All Rights Reserved

The original purchaser of this book has permission to reproduce this song for educational use in one school only. Any other use is strictly prohibited.

Teacher Tips

When to Use the Song
This song is perfect to sing at the end of the day or as students walk out the door.

Rule/Procedure
Saying goodbye

Similar Songs
#5   Buenos Dias

#19   Hello

#30   Please and Thank You

#44   When You Say "Hello"

#45   When You Use Good Manners

Musical Activities
• Practice singing the song with the suggested motions.

• Perform the song at various tempos, and then, let students decide which tempo they enjoy the most.

Cross-Curricular Activities
Reading/Language Arts
"Toodle-Oodle-Oo" is a nonsense word that can mean goodbye. Identify other nonsense words for the words "goodbye" and "hello."

Writing
Have students write a story about a time when they had to say goodbye. Write about how that made them feel.

Math
Have the class perform this song at a very slow tempo, at a moderate tempo and at a very fast tempo. Assign a few students to serve as timekeepers and record the amount of time for each performance. Have students calculate the difference in time between the fastest and slowest performance.

Social Studies
Learn to say goodbye in other languages.

Art
Have students design a greeting card that says "goodbye" or "missing you."

41. WALK, DON'T RUN!

(4-measure introduction on recording)

Words and Music by BRAD GREEN

Copyright © 2009 by HAL LEONARD CORPORATION
International Copyright Secured All Rights Reserved

Teacher Tips

When to Use the Song
Remind students to walk instead of run. As with most classroom management, the management must be done before the event. In this example, it is too late to sing the song if the students are already running; therefore, anticipate running, and sing the song before any running takes place.

Rule/Procedure
Walking instead of running

Similar Songs
#2   Be Careful
#13 Find a Partner
#17 Go Back to Your Place
#34 Show Respect
#43 When You Need to Move Around the Room

Musical Activities
Have students feel the steady beat in a variety of ways such as stepping the beat, tapping different parts of the body, waving, snapping, and so forth, while performing the song.

Cross-Curricular Activities
Reading/Language Arts
In this song, the word "walk" is repeated three times for emphasis. Have students identify other words that are often repeated in language for emphasis.

Writing
When the beginning sound of a word is repeated for emphasis, it is called alliteration. For example, "Wild waltzing walruses want waffles." Have students write sentences with alliterations that begin with the letter "w" or other letters of the alphabet.

Math
Help students determine the time differences between walking and running a certain distance.

Social Studies
Present and discuss the statements: "People walk less today than they did 100 year ago." What things have contributed to this change?

Science/Health:
Teach students how to measure their heart rate. Then, have them measure their heart rate after thirty seconds of resting, thirty seconds of walking, and thirty seconds of running.

Art
Have students draw the same animal in two different positions: walking and running.

42. WASH YOUR HANDS

Gospel Rock (♩ = 138)

Words and Music by BRAD GREEN

Wash your hands to get them clean. Wa-ter, soap, scrub is the rou - tine.

Wash un - til they're squeek - y clean. Wash them well for good hy-giene!

Wash them well for good hy - giene! Wash them well for

good hy - giene! Wash your hands!

 **Teacher Tips**

When to Use the Song

This song can be sung before going to lunch, after any messy activity, or anytime students need to clean their hands.

Rule/Procedure

Good hygiene

Similar Songs

#7   Clean Up!

#45   When You Use Good Manners

Musical Activities

- Have students create movements or actions to this song.

- As a memory exercise, have the students clap the rhythm of the words while singing the words silently inside their heads. Next, have them clap the rhythm of each phrase one at a time.

Cross-Curricular Activities

Reading/Language Arts

Make a list of synonyms (or anonyms) of the words "clean" and "dirty." Compare the lists.

Math

Compare the prices of different hand soaps. Analyze the results.

Social Studies

Discuss ways that students can help prevent spreading germs in the school community and/or in their homes.

Science

Learn more about Louis Pasteur (1822–1895), the French scientist who made breakthroughs in germ theory and the prevention of disease.

Physical Education/Health

Discuss and model the correct way to wash your hands. Discuss how washing hands prevents the spreading of germs.

43. WHEN YOU NEED TO MOVE AROUND THE ROOM

(7-measure introduction on recording)

Words and Music by BRAD GREEN

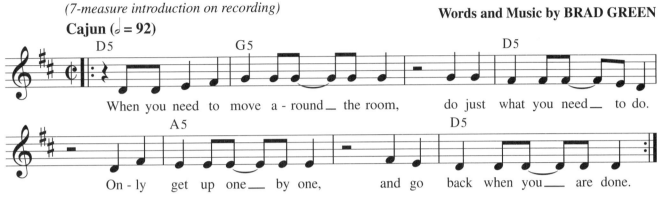

Cajun (♩ = 92)

When you need to move a - round the room, do just what you need to do.

On - ly get up one by one, and go back when you are done.

 **Teacher Tips**

When to Use the Song
Sing the song to remind students the procedure for moving around the room.

Rule/Procedure
Moving around the classroom with purpose

Similar Songs
#10   Do You Have What You Need?

#15   Get Ready to Start the Day

#29   Move in 5-4-3-2-1

#37   Stay in Your Seat

#38   Take Turns

Musical Activities
- Discuss *ostinato* (a recurring melodic or rhythmic fragment). Have students compose a rhythmic *ostinato* to accompany this song.
- First, perform the *ostinato* with body percussion (stomping, patting legs, snapping, clapping, and so forth), and then on rhythm instruments.

Cross-Curricular Activities
Reading/Language Arts
Reinforce this procedure by playing a reading game. Write a sentence on the board. Write the individual words in the sentence on cards. Place the word cards in different parts of the room. Have students follow the procedure in the song (getting out of their seats one at a time) to find the word cards and then arranging the cards in sentence order.

Writing
Have students imagine a story that occurs in different parts of the room. Use this as a prompt to start writing.

Math
Measure different items in the room. Working in partners, have students discuss the procedure for measuring each item.

Social Studies
Identify people in your school that help you "do just what you need to do," like the nurse, the counselor, the cafeteria staff, the librarian, to name a few. Identify people in the local community who help you "do just what you need to do." *(policemen, firemen, librarians, and so forth).*

Science
Discuss appropriate ways to move around the room when moving from seats to work on a science experiment in a different area of the room.

44. WHEN YOU SAY "HELLO"

Words and Music by BRAD GREEN

Moderate 2-beat (♩ = 132)

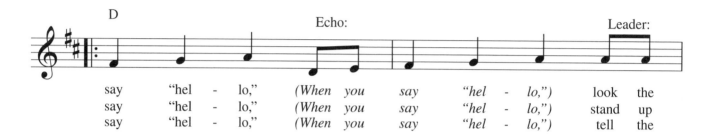

say "hel - lo," (When you say "hel - lo,") look the
say "hel - lo," (When you say "hel - lo,") stand up
say "hel - lo," (When you say "hel - lo,") tell the

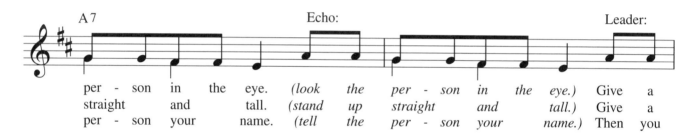

per - son in the eye. (look the per - son in the eye.) Give a
straight and tall. (stand up straight and tall.) Give a
per - son your name. (tell the per - son your name.) Then you

nice warm smile. (Give a nice warm smile.) Say "hel-
firm hand shake. (Give a firm hand shake,) not
lis - ten close, (Then you lis - ten close,) while they

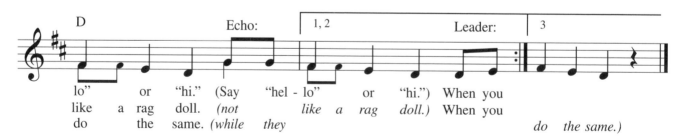

lo" or "hi." (Say "hel - lo" or "hi.") When you
like a rag doll. (not like a rag doll.) When you
do the same. (while they do the same.)

Copyright © 2009 by HAL LEONARD CORPORATION
International Copyright Secured   All Rights Reserved

Teacher Tips

When to Use the Song
Greeting another person properly is an important life skill—one that should be taught and practiced.

Rule/Procedure
Greeting another person

Brief Version
Sing the first verse only

Similar Songs
#5   Buenos Dias

#18   The Golden Rule

#19   Hello

#24   Life Is Better With a Friend

#33   Say Your Name

#34   Show Respect

#45   When You Use Good Manners

Musical Activities
- After the song is very familiar, have volunteers sing the "Leader" part.
- Have students make up actions to the song while singing.

Cross-Curricular Activities

Reading/Language Arts
This song is written in the style of call and response. Present a short poem in a call and response format. Have a selected student read a line of the poem, and have the class repeat the line as a response. Have different students serve as leaders/readers.

Writing
Encourage students to imagine a scene in which they meet their favorite hero for the very first time. Write about the scene, the hero, and the dialogue between the two.

Math
Have the students count the number of times they sing a response in this song. *(4)*

Social Studies
Working in partners, have students role-model ways to greet people. Have students determine which greetings are proper and which ones are not.

Science
Discuss the five senses. After reading *My Five Senses* by Aliki, decide which of the senses are used when greeting another person.

Art
Draw a picture of two people saying hello to each other in a proper manner.

45. WHEN YOU USE GOOD MANNERS

(2-measure drum introduction on recording)

Words and Music by BRAD GREEN

Relaxed (♩ = 88)

(2nd time: add hand claps on beats 2 and 4)

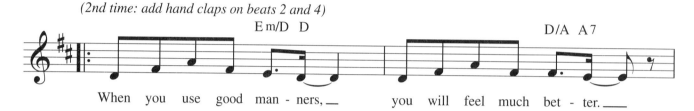

When you use good man - ners, ___ you will feel much bet - ter. ___

(end claps)

You will make friends eas - i - er, and be - come a lead - er. ___

You will be res - pec - ted. ___ You will be re - fined.

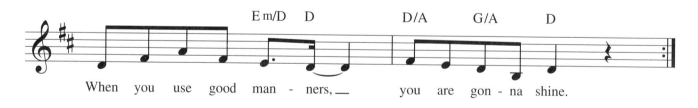

When you use good man - ners, ___ you are gon - na shine.

You are gon - na shine. You are gon - na shine!

 Teacher Tips

When to Use the Song
This song teaches the benefits of using good manners—an important reminder.

Rule/Procedure
Using good manners

Brief Version
Sing the first four measures.

Similar Songs
#4   Before You Speak, Raise Your Hand

#30 Please and Thank You

#34 Show Respect

#38 Take Turns

Musical Activities
- Have students improvise or compose a rhythmic accompaniment to this song.
- Determine which phrases are the same and which phrases are different. Discuss ways to label the form of this song, and then do so.

Cross-Curricular Activities

Reading/Language Arts
Have students identify good manners that may be used in everyday conversation.

Writing
Make a list of good manners that should be practiced.

Math
Discuss ways that one can exercise good manners during math class.

Social Studies
People often have different ideas about what constitutes good manners. Identify some reasons why there are varying opinions about good and bad manners.

Science
Discuss the importance of using good manners when taking care of the environment.

Physical Education/Health
Some good manners promote better health. Make a list of these (covering the mouth when coughing, for example).

46. YOU'LL NEED YOUR (BOOK) FOR THIS ACTIVITY

(2-measure introduction on recording)

Energetically (♩ = 126)

Words and Music by BRAD GREEN

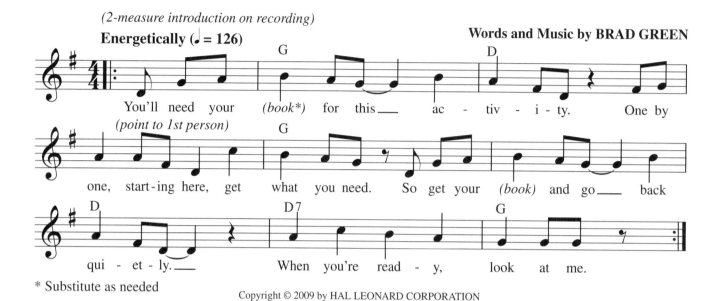

You'll need your (book*) for this ___ ac - tiv - i - ty. One by

(point to 1st person)

one, start-ing here, get what you need. So get your (book) and go ___ back

qui - et - ly. ___ When you're read - y, look at me.

* Substitute as needed

 **Teacher Tips**

When to Use the Song
Sing this song when students need to go somewhere else in the room to get materials or supplies. Repeat the song until students have what they need.

Rule/Procedure
Getting supplies/materials one by one

Similar Songs
#10 Do You Have What You Need?

#35 A Song to Pass Things Out

#38 Take Turns

Musical Activities
- Replace the word "book" with any materials that the students need to gather.
- At the end of the song, check to see if every student is looking at the teacher/singer. If not, repeat the last phrase until everyone is looking at the teacher/singer.

Cross-Curricular Activities
Reading/Language Arts
Make a list of the materials or supplies that a good reader needs.

Writing
Imagine the tools, supplies or materials that are needed to complete a particular job. Use this as a prompt to write about a certain job.

Math
Have students identify four different supplies in their desks. Determine the number of times they use each supply during the day. Rank the four supplies in order of the most used to least used.

Social Studies
Have students discuss a career of interest, and then determine the tools that are used in that career.

Science
Discuss how technology is a tool for learning.

Art
Find a tool that students have never used before and use it to create a work of art.

CLASSIFIED INDEX

Good Behavior (continued)

Goodbye/Lesson Closers

Greetings

Lesson Openers

Quieting a Class

Personal Space

Procedures

Self Esteem

Singing Games/ Cross-Curricular Games

Sit Down

Sharing

Using Caution

CD TRACK LISTING

Performance/ Accompaniment	Title
1/2	Always Share
3/4	Be Careful
5/6	Be Still
7/8	Before You Speak, Raise Your Hand
9/10	Buenos Dias
11/12	Clap One Time If You Can Hear My Voice
13/14	Clean Up!
15/16	Come to Attention
17/18	Criss-Cross Applesauce
19/20	Do You Have What You Need?
21/22	Don't Forget Your Homework
23/24	Everybody Listen
25/26	Find a Partner
27/28	Follow the Instructions
29/30	Get Ready to Start the Day
31/32	Give Me the Magic Five!
33/34	Go Back to Your Place
35/36	The Golden Rule
37/38	Hello
39/40	Hocus Pocus, Everybody Focus
41/42	It's OK to Have Different Feelings
43/44	It's Time to Say Goodbye
45/46	Keep Your Hands to Yourself
47/48	Life Is Better With a Friend
49/50	Make a Choice
51/52	Make a Circle
53/54	Make a Line
55/56	Marshmallow Mouth
57/58	Move in 5-4-3-2-1
59/60	Please and Thank You
61/62	Polka Dot Spot
63/64	Rules Song
65/66	Say Your Name
67/68	Show Respect
69/70	A Song to Pass Things Out
71/72	Stand Up, Sit Down
73/74	Stay in Your Seat
75/76	Take Turns
77/78	There Are Two Minutes Left
79/80	Toodle-Oodle-Oo
81/82	Walk, Don't Run!
83/84	Wash Your Hands
85/86	When You Need to Move Around the Room
87/88	When You Say "Hello"
89/90	When You Use Good Manners
91/92	You'll Need Your (Book) for This Activity